Best of Rancid for Bass

Transcribed by Steve Gorenberg

Cherry Lane Music Company

Director of Publications/Project Editor: Mark Phillips

ISBN 978-1-57560-792-4

Copyright © 2005 Cherry Lane Music Company
International Copyright Secured   All Rights Reserved

The music, text, design and graphics in this publication are protected by copyright law. Any duplication or transmission,
by any means, electronic, mechanical, photocopying, recording or otherwise, is an infringement of copyright.

Visit our website at www.cherrylane.com

RANCID

First of all, Rancid are the real deal, and *no one* lives and breathes punk rock like Tim Armstrong, Lars Frederiksen, Matt Freeman, and Brett Reed, who've always stayed true to their DIY roots: Three Chords and the Truth. They've toured extensively worldwide and have broken ground and blazed trails for numerous bands and artists. They set the standard—before Green Day.

But let's go back to 1987...

Matt and Tim form Operation Ivy. Op Ivy, who influenced Green Day and countless others, is the most-recognized and critically acclaimed East Bay punk band of all time. (Green Day's first punk show was with Op Ivy at Gilman St.) The Op Ivy record is past gold and is still a much sought-after record.

Now speed ahead a few years to:

1993
RANCID, the first record, is recorded at the Epitaph home studio, Westbeach, with Tim, Matt, and Brett. Enter Lars Frederiksen, who joins right after the band is formed in February. They make a video for "Hyena," which gets played on MTV; the band tours and tours. The record is critically acclaimed, and a hell of a lot of fanzines say that this record put punk rock back on the map.

1994
LET'S GO is produced by Brett Gurewitz! The band has five days to make a record and they end up recording *23 songs*. Also critically acclaimed across the board! The band makes videos for "Nihilism" and "Salvation," which receive a lot of play on MTV; the songs also do well as radio singles. The band continues to tour the States and around the world.

1995
...AND OUT COME THE WOLVES is recorded with Jerry Finn. It's the band's bestselling record and continues to sell boatloads. Picked by *Rolling Stone* and *Spin* as one of the *essential* records of all time. The band makes videos for "Time Bomb" and "Ruby Soho" and both do very well as radio singles. The record makes quite a few Top 10 lists that year and *Spin* votes them one of the most influential bands. In fact, for two years in a row, 1995 and '96, Rancid is voted as one of the Most Influential Bands in *Spin*. The band tours around the world and in November '95 play *Saturday Night Live* as featured musical guest. At the end of '96, after about three years of touring and three records with some 60 sides, they take a break and begin recording different sessions in about five different studios in Kingston, Jamaica; New Orleans; New York City; the Bay Area; and L.A. Those songs make up the *Life Won't Wait* record.

1998
LIFE WON'T WAIT grabs a 4-star review in *Rolling Stone*. The band tours internationally. The record features musical contributions from a huge number of talented friends of the band—a critical milestone for the band that really showcases their awesome songwriting and might. To this day the band pulls out some of those tunes on the road and they never fail to please and inspire new fans.

2000
RANCID (V) is produced by Brett Gurewitz. Kind of back to the early Rancid sound and reminiscent of *Let's Go* and the first record, it makes the hardcore punks very happy. The band plays their biggest tour to date, including the Reading Festival and Japan, and are on the cover of KERRANG'S *bestselling* issue of all time. The band headlines the Warped Tour and right afterwards have their biggest headlining tour to date.

2003
INDESTRUCTIBLE is produced by Brett Gurewitz. Lars and Tim have written more songs together for this record than any other previous release. The record is *punk!* It's lyrically and musically upside your head. It includes brilliant songwriting and sing-along choruses reminiscent of *...And Out Come the Wolves*.

CONTENTS

- 4 **Axiom**
- 9 **David Courtney**
- 15 **Detroit**
- 19 **Django**
- 27 **Fall Back Down**
- 34 **Journey to the End of the East Bay**
- 39 **Life Won't Wait**
- 45 **Maxwell Murder**
- 48 **Old Friend**
- 52 **Radio Havana**
- 57 **Red Hot Moon**
- 63 **Roots Radicals**
- 68 **Side Kick**
- 72 **Time Bomb**
- 76 **White Knuckle Ride**

- 80 *Bass Notation Legend*

AXIOM

Words and Music by Tim Armstrong,
Lars Frederiksen and Matt Freeman

Copyright © 2000 You're A Rattlesnake (ASCAP)
All Rights Administered by Wixen Music Publishing, Inc.
International Copyright Secured   All Rights Reserved

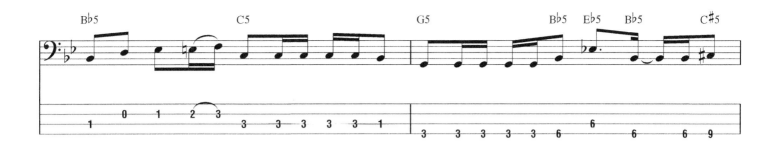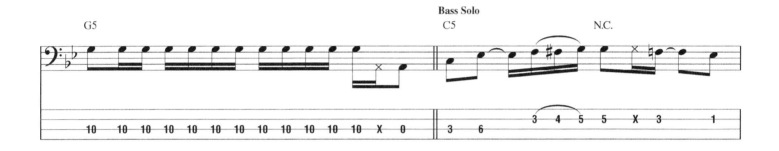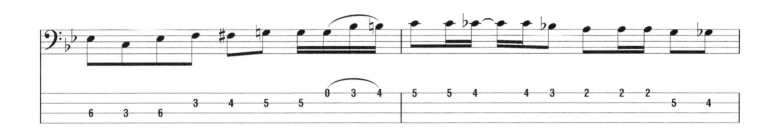

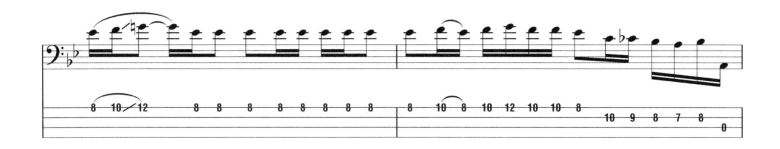
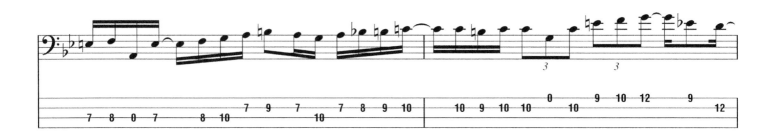
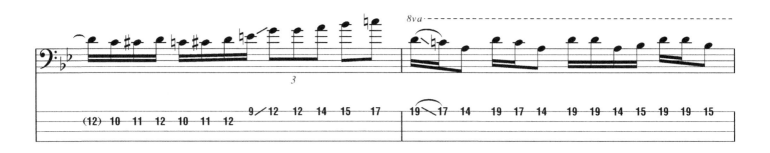
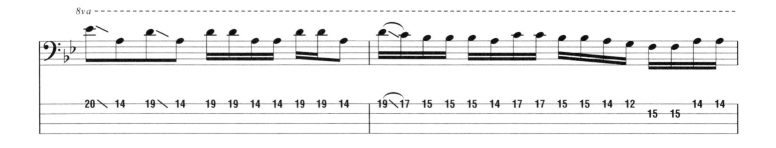
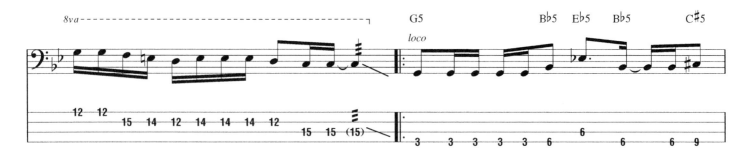
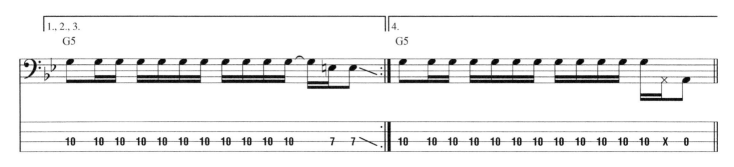

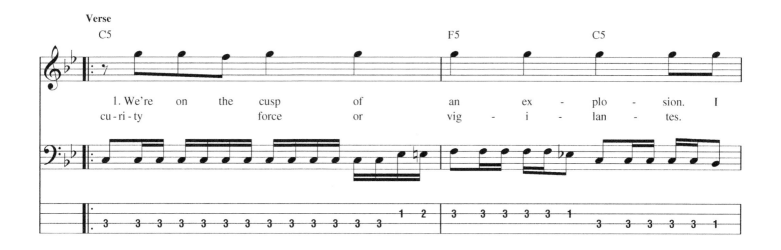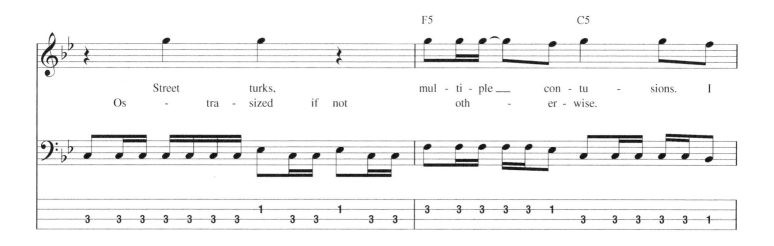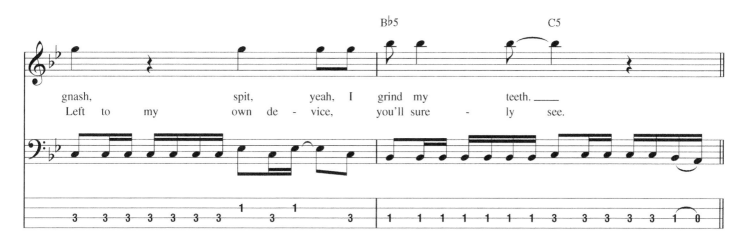

DAVID COURTNEY

Words and Music by
Tim Armstrong and Lars Frederiksen

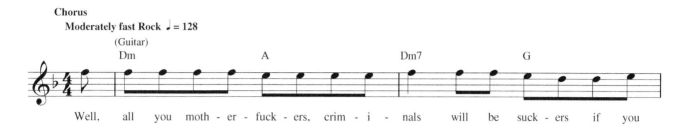
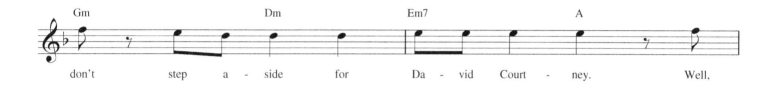
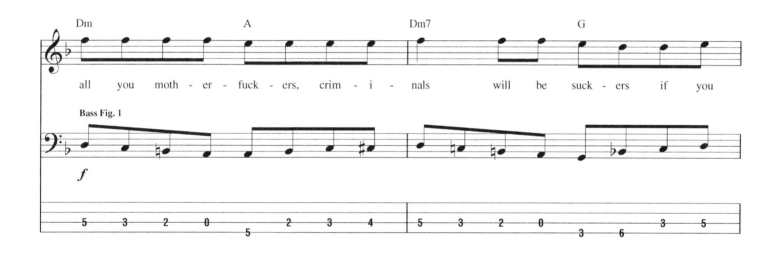
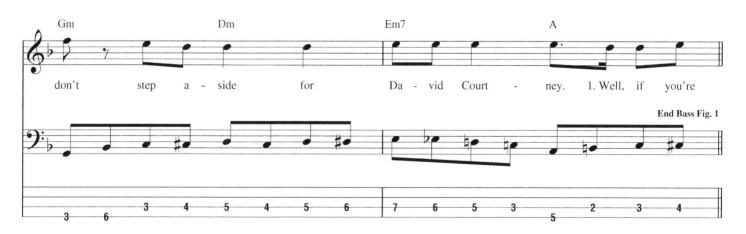

Copyright © 2003 You're A Rattlesnake (ASCAP)
All Rights Administered by Wixen Music Publishing, Inc.
International Copyright Secured   All Rights Reserved

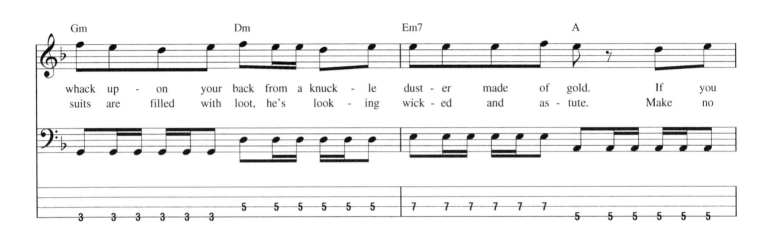
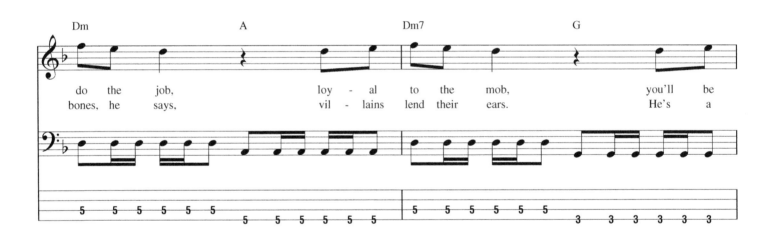
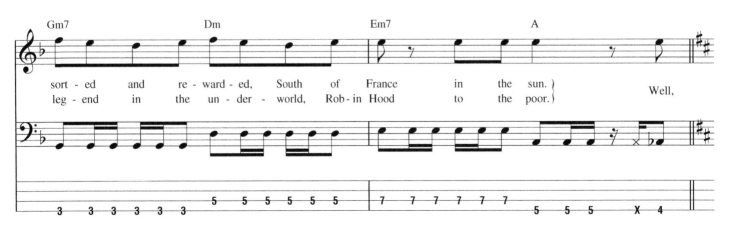

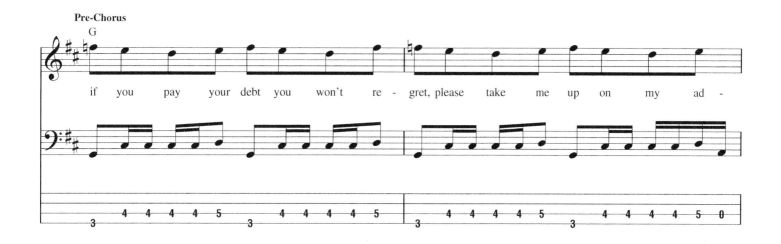
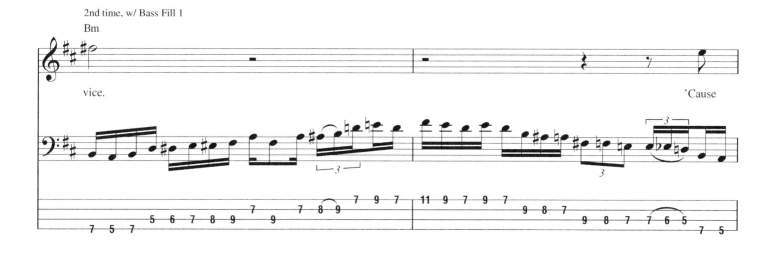
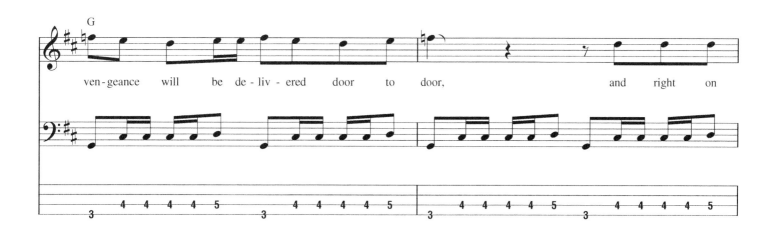

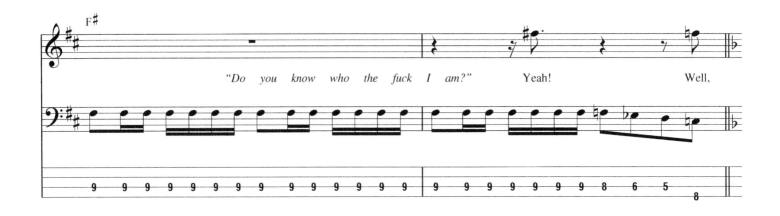
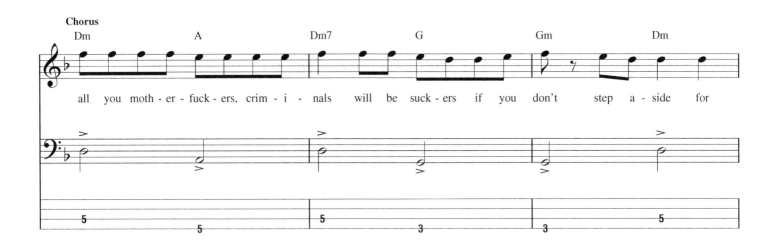
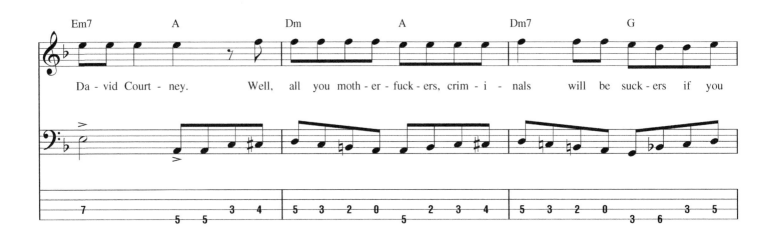

DETROIT

Words and Music by
Tim Armstrong and Roger Freeman

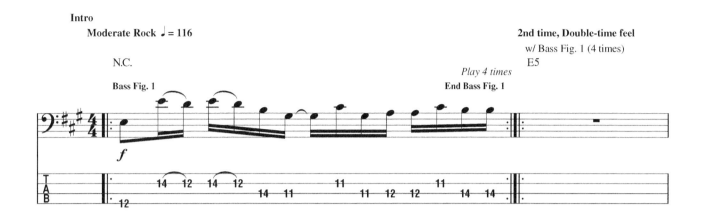

Copyright © 1995 Rancid Music (ASCAP)
All Rights Administered by Wixen Music Publishing, Inc.
International Copyright Secured All Rights Reserved

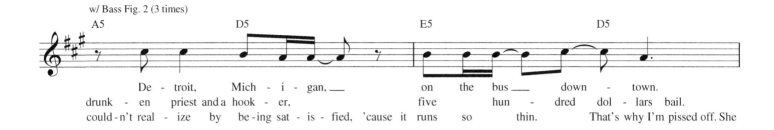
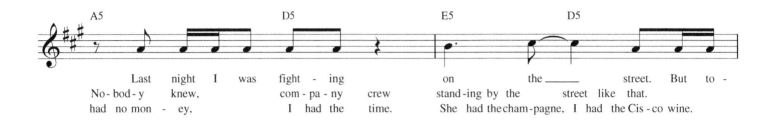

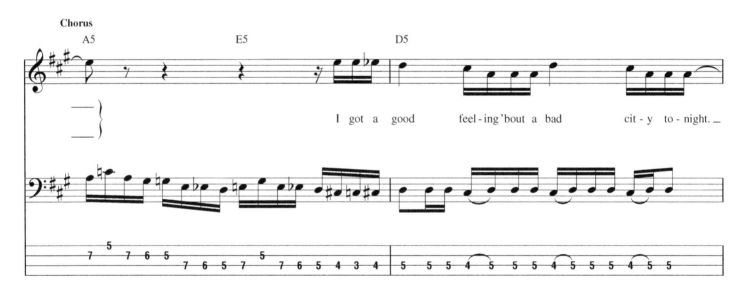
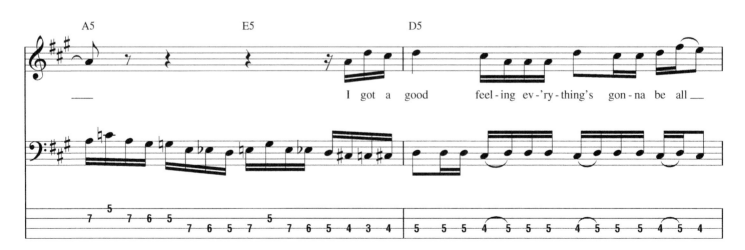

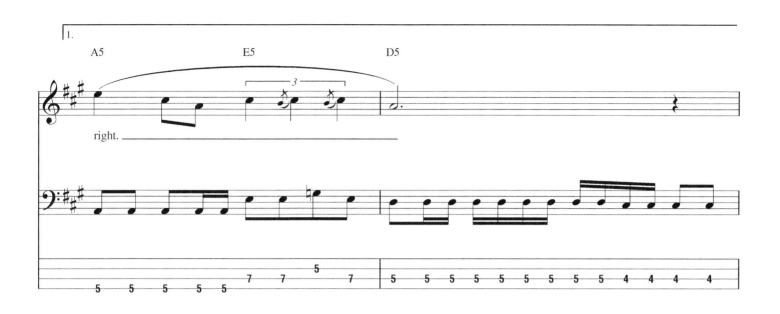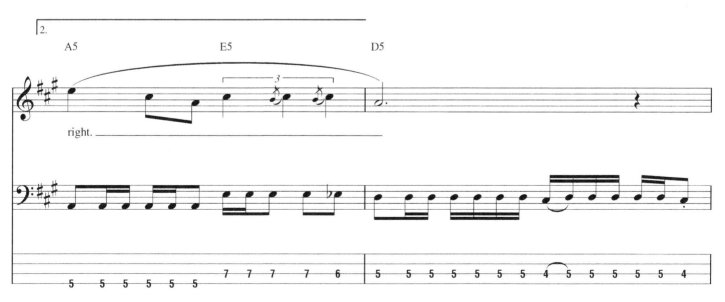

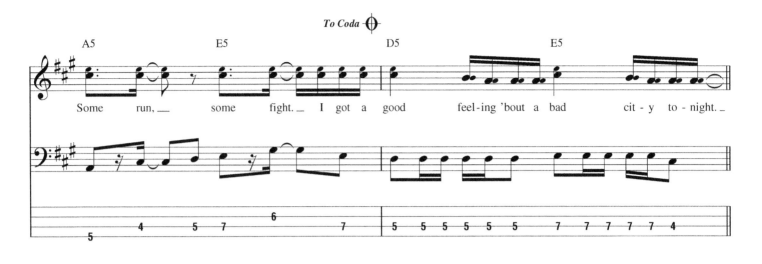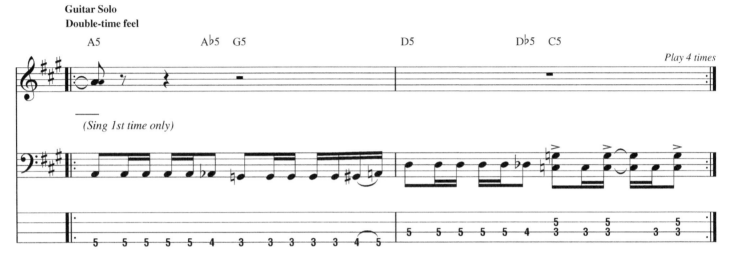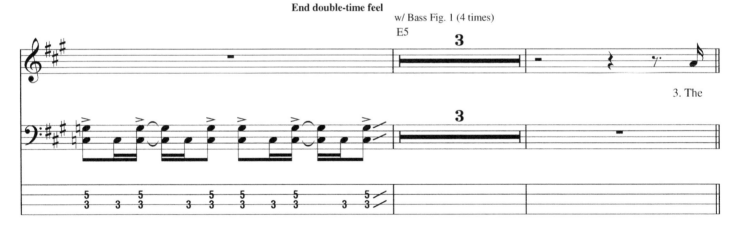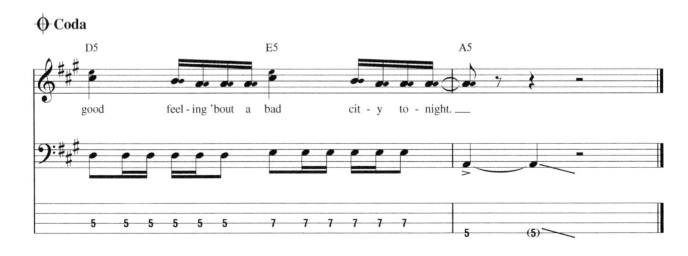

DJANGO

Words and Music by
Tim Armstrong

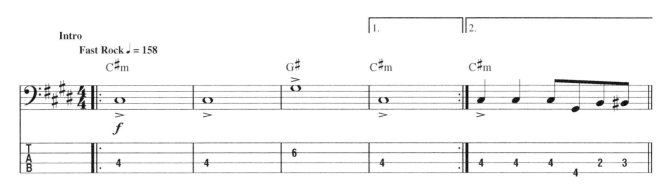

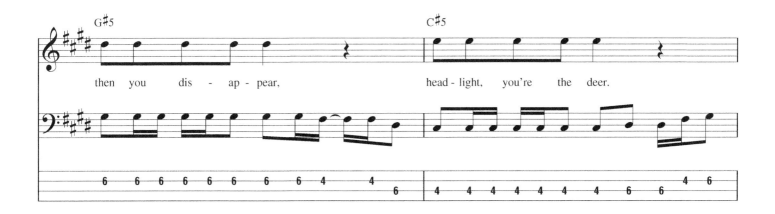
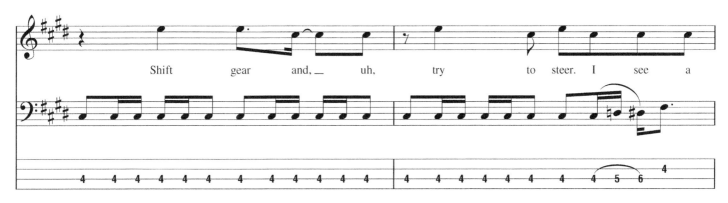

Copyright © 2003 You're A Rattlesnake (ASCAP)
All Rights Administered by Wixen Music Publishing, Inc.
International Copyright Secured   All Rights Reserved

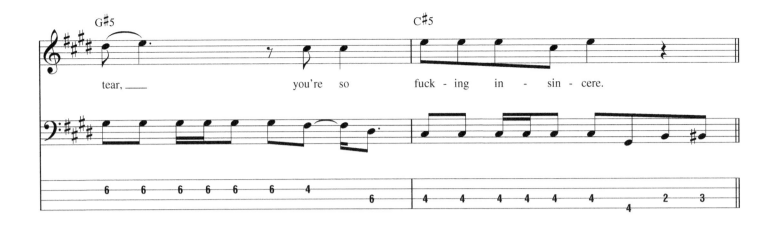

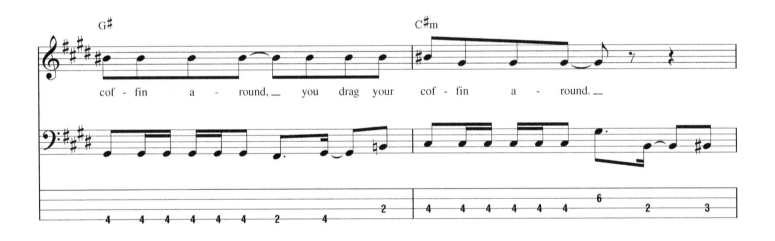

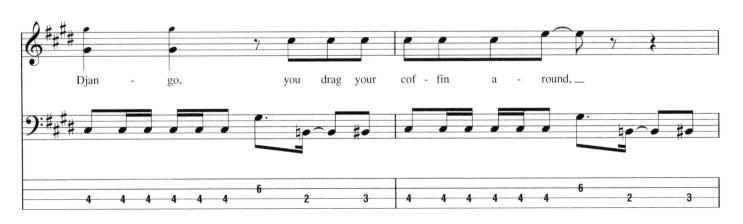

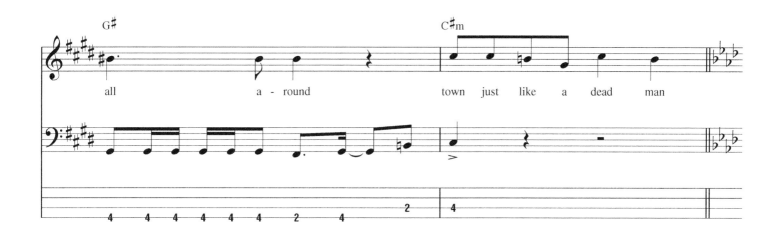
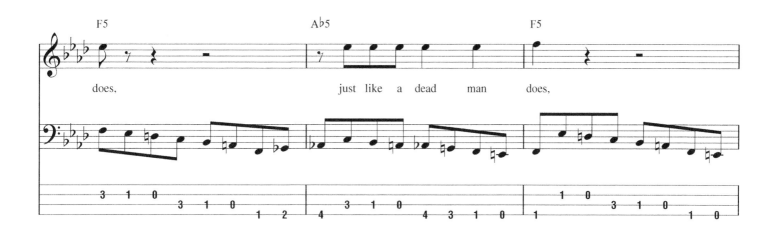
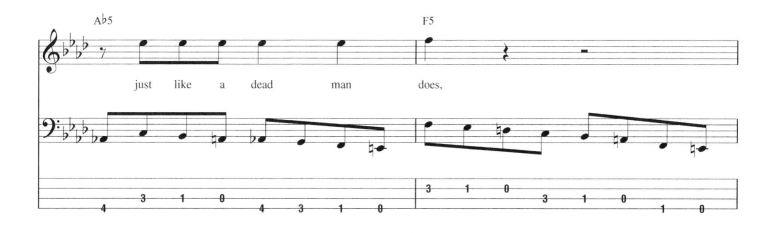
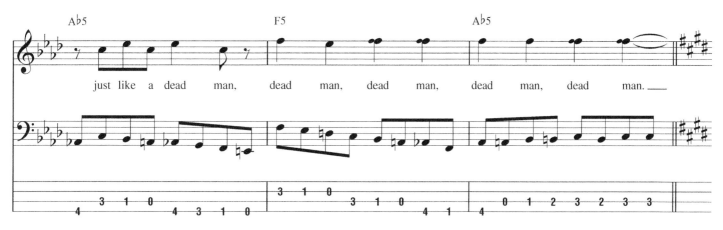

23

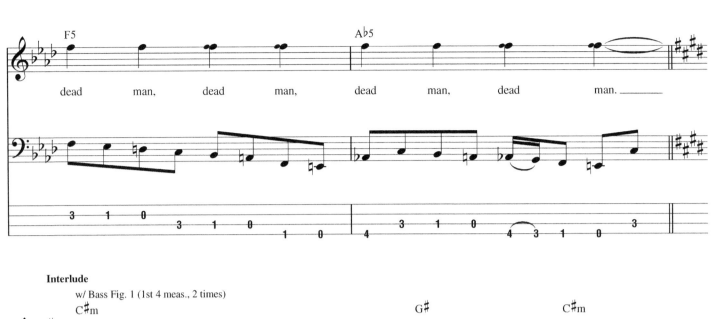

Interlude

Guitar Solo
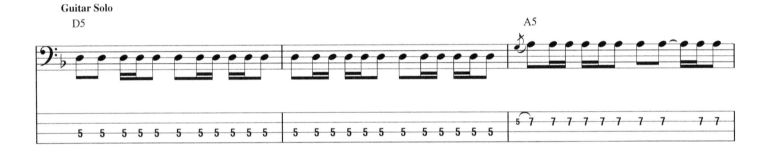

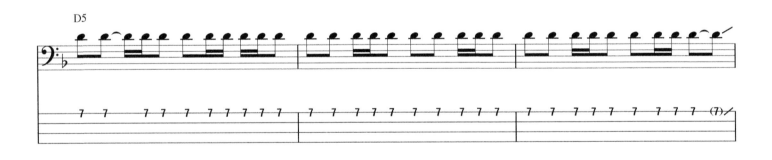

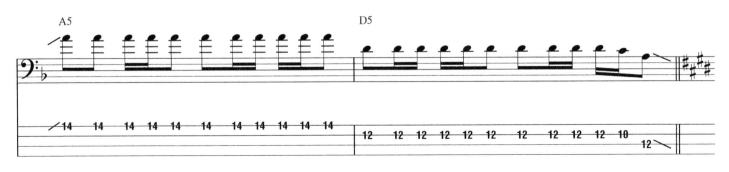

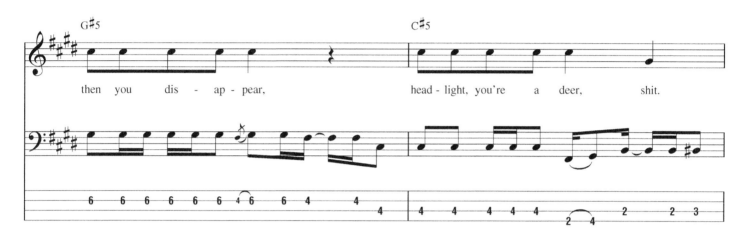
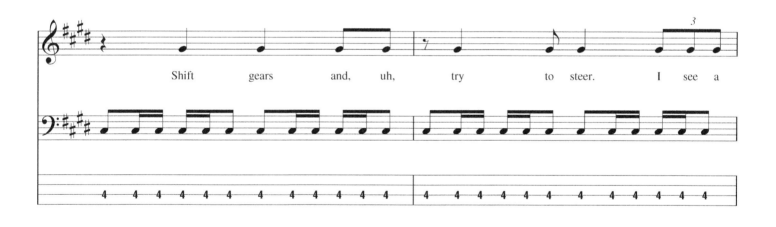
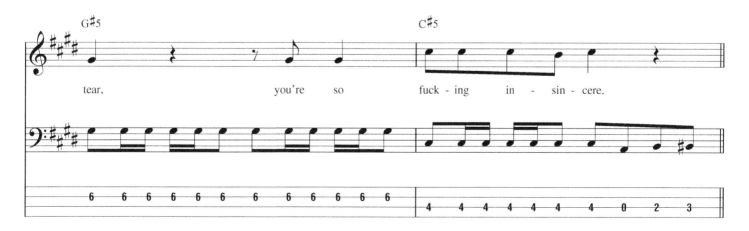

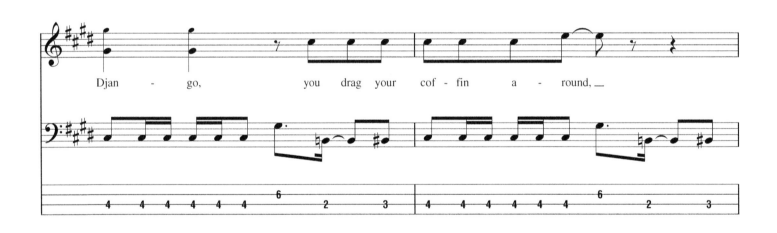

FALL BACK DOWN

Words and Music by
Tim Armstrong and Lars Frederiksen

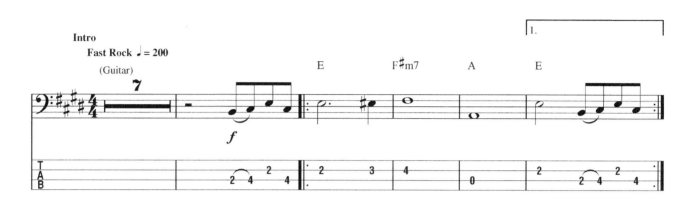

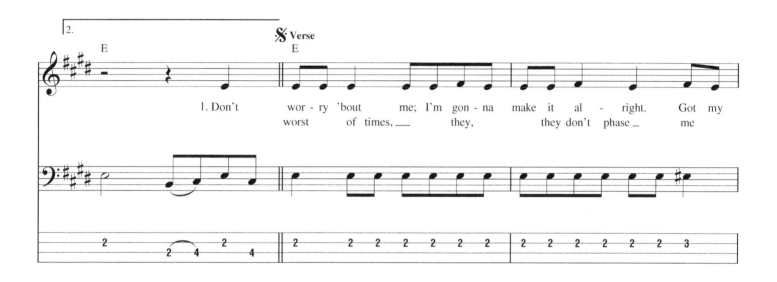

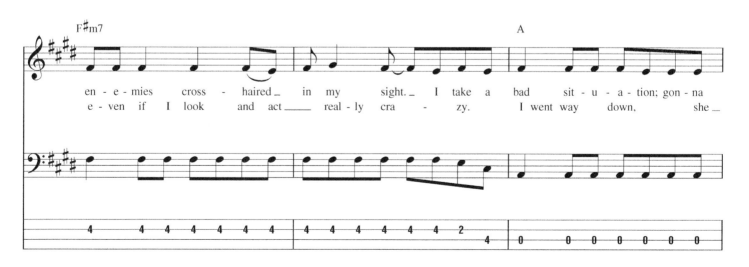

Copyright © 2003 You're A Rattlesnake (ASCAP)
All Rights Administered by Wixen Music Publishing, Inc.
International Copyright Secured All Rights Reserved

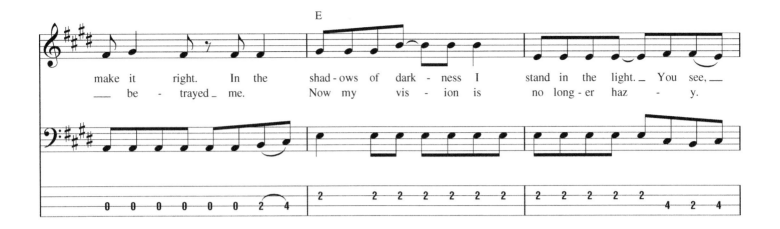
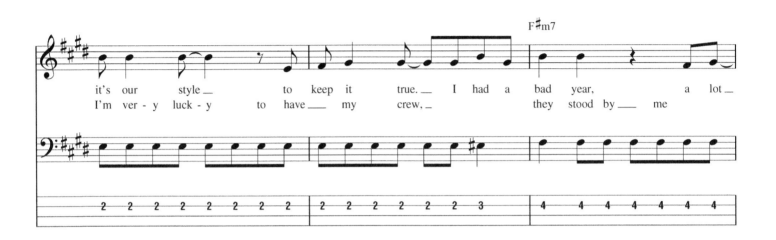
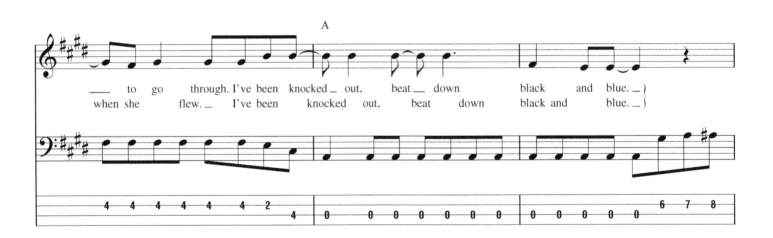
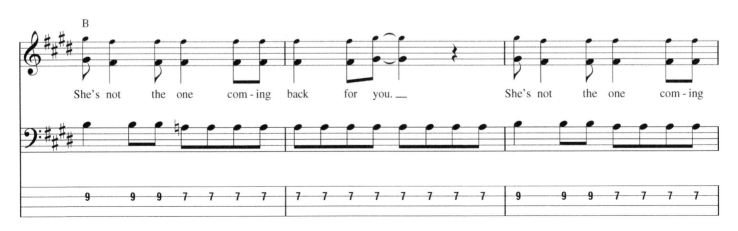

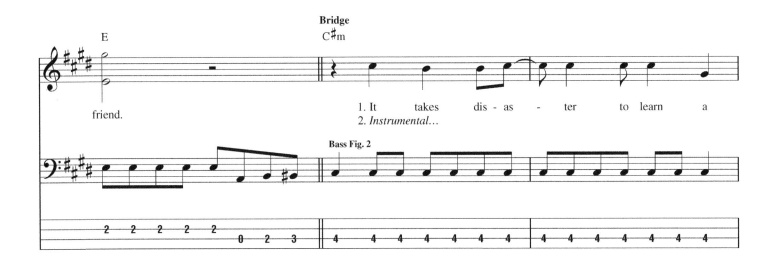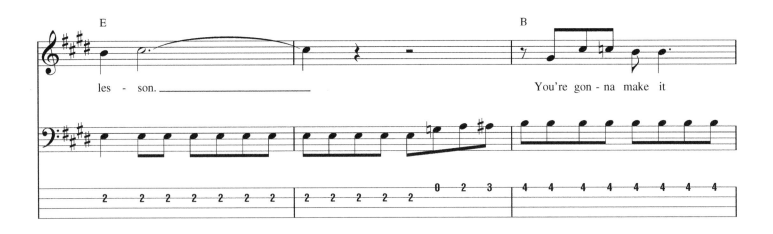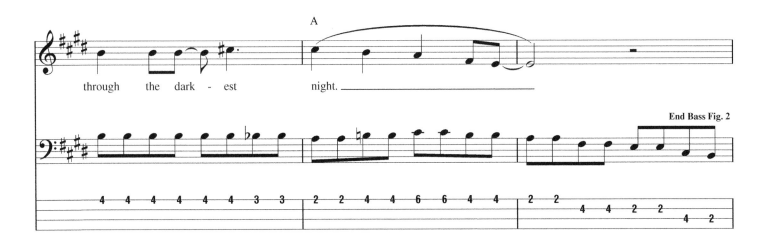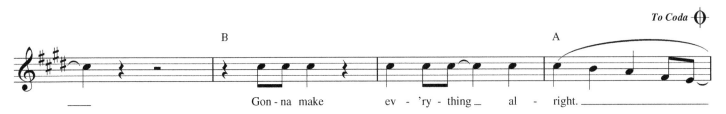

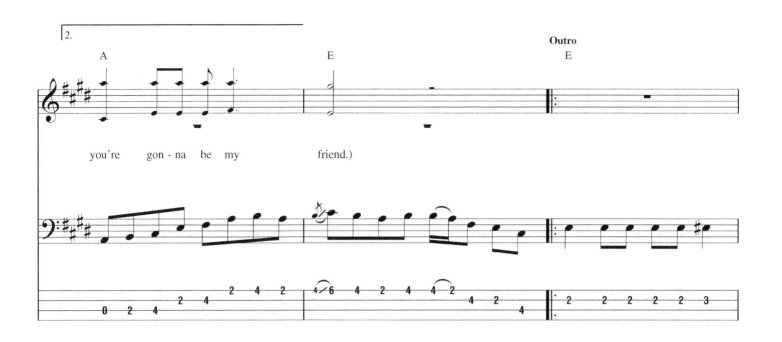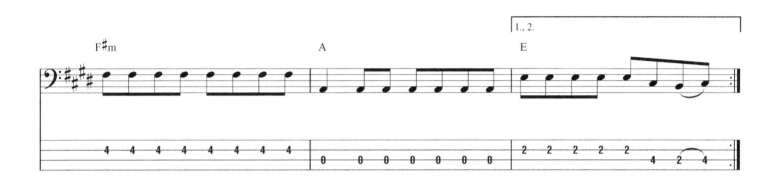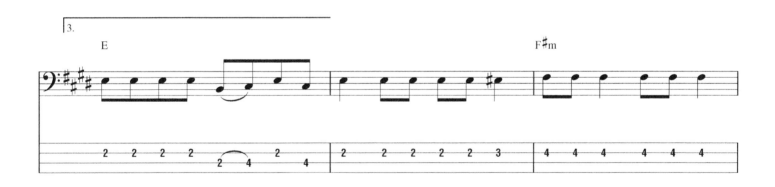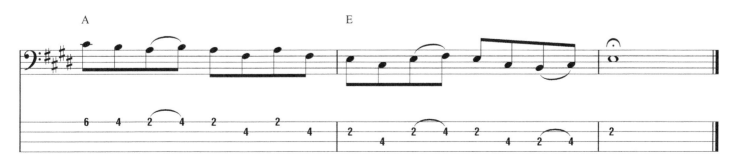

JOURNEY TO THE END OF THE EAST BAY

Words and Music by Tim Armstrong, Matt Freeman and Lars Frederiksen

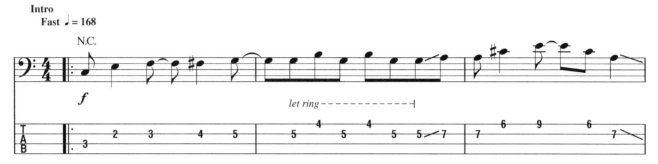

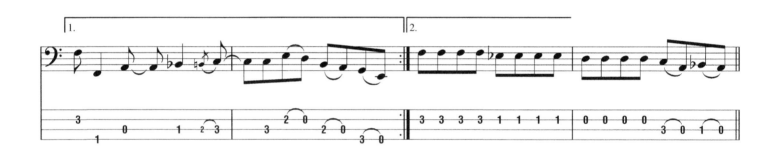
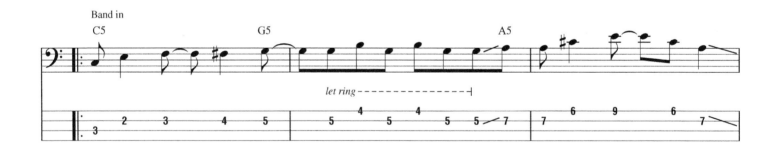

Copyright © 1995 I Want To Go Where The Action Is Music (BMI)
All Rights Administered by Wixen Music Publishing, Inc.
International Copyright Secured   All Rights Reserved

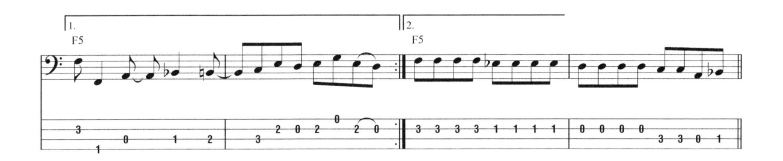

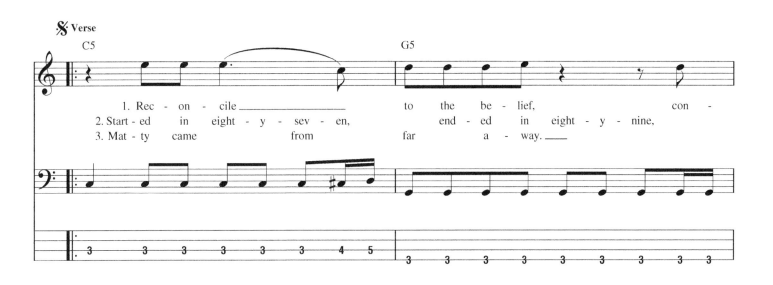

1. Rec - on - cile _____ to the be - lief, con-
2. Start - ed in eight - y - sev - en, end - ed in eight - y - nine,
3. Mat - ty came from far a - way. _____

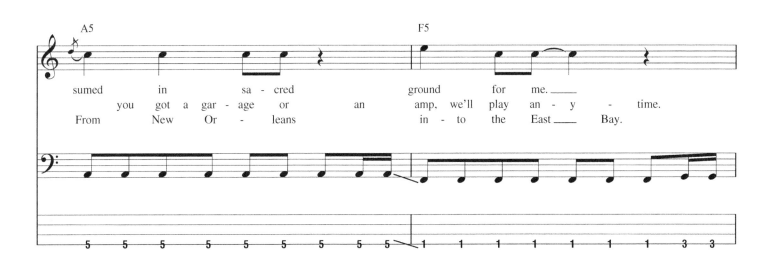

sumed in sa - cred ground for me. _____
you got a gar - age or an amp, we'll play an - y - time.
From New Or - leans in - to the East _____ Bay.

There was - n't al - ways a place to go, but there was
It was just the four of us, yeah man, the core of us.
He said, "This is a Mec - ca." _____ I said, "This

35

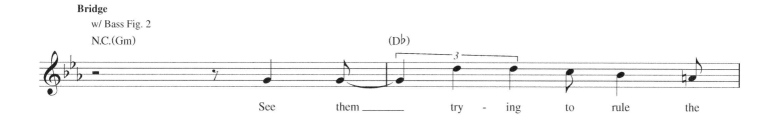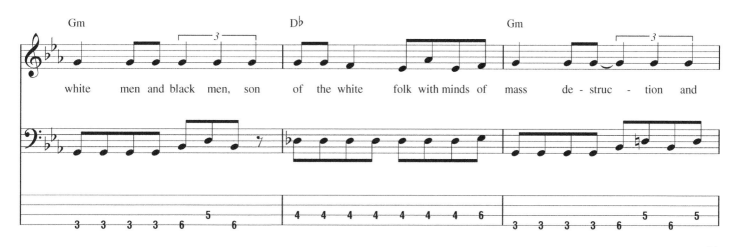

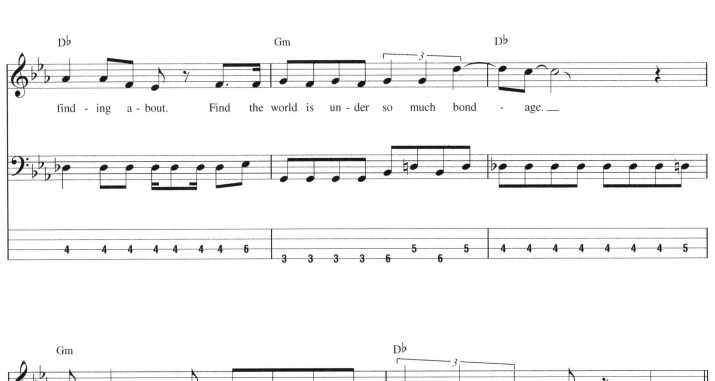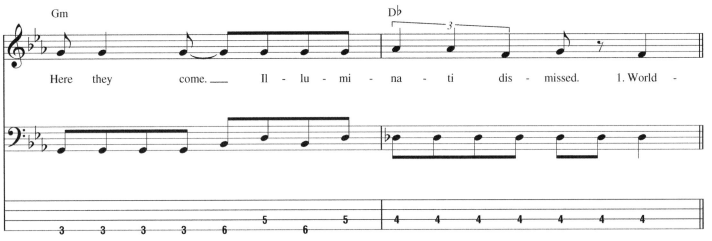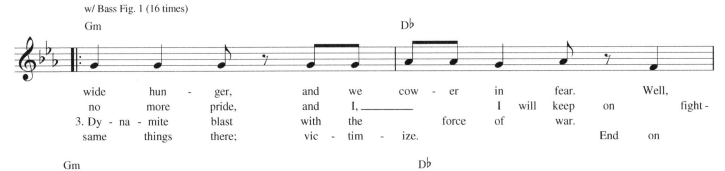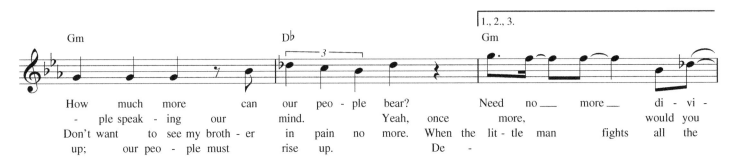

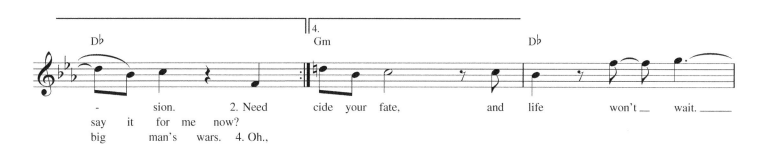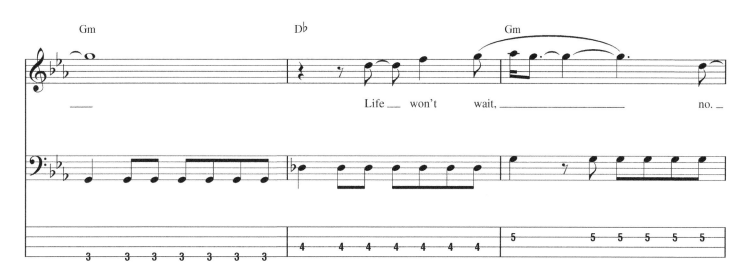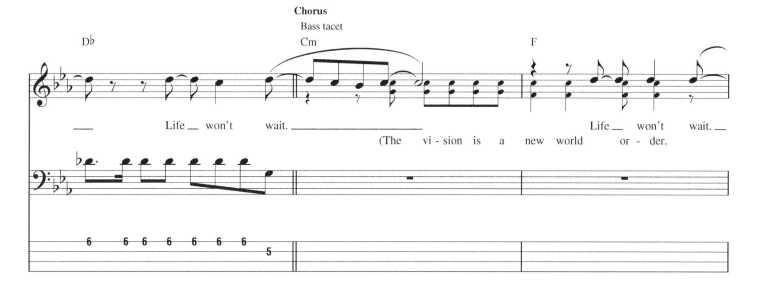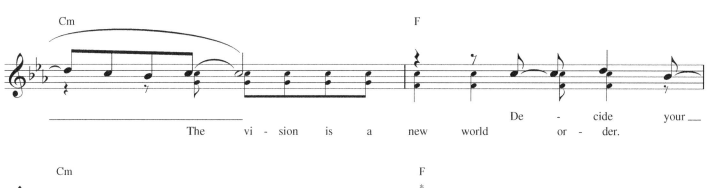

*w/ additional Reggae-style vocal ad lib till end.

MAXWELL MURDER

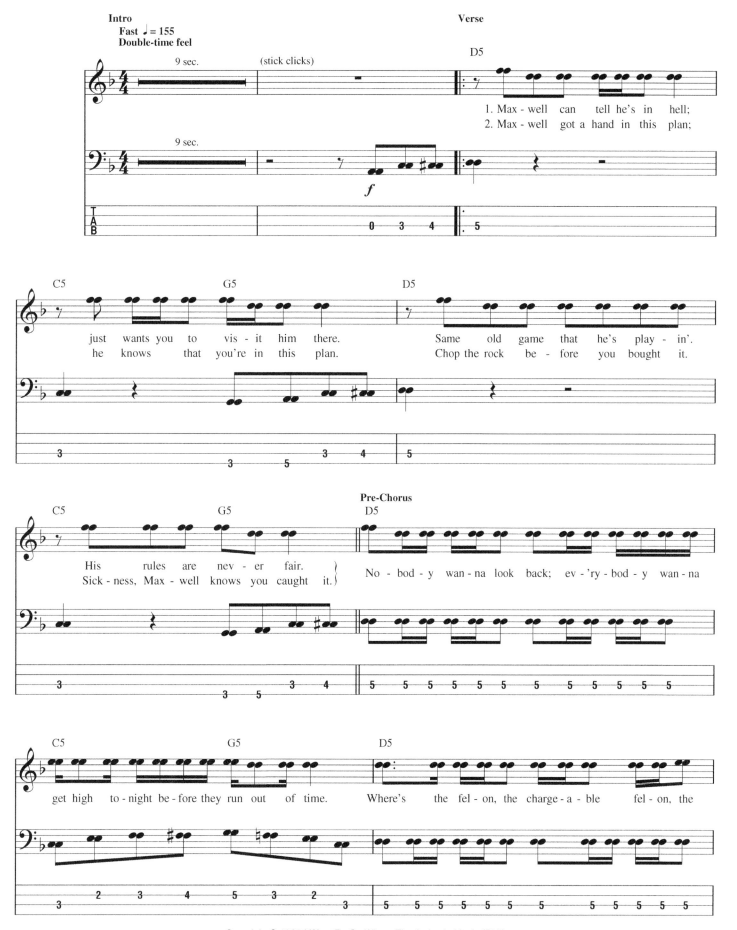

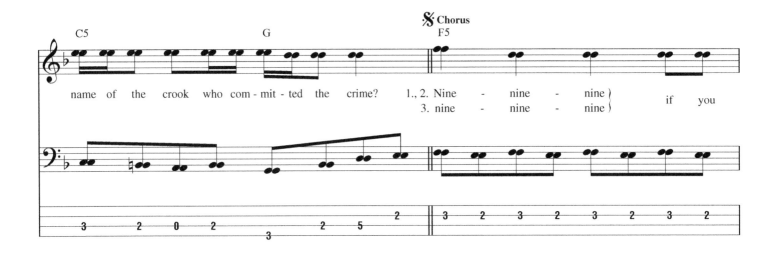
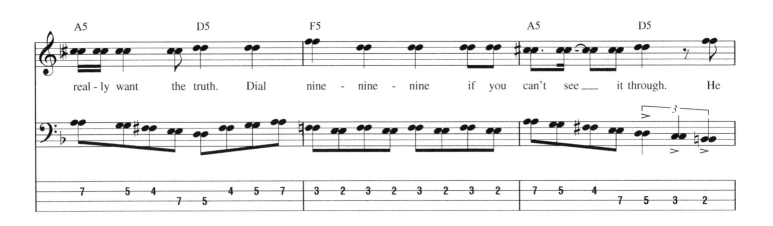
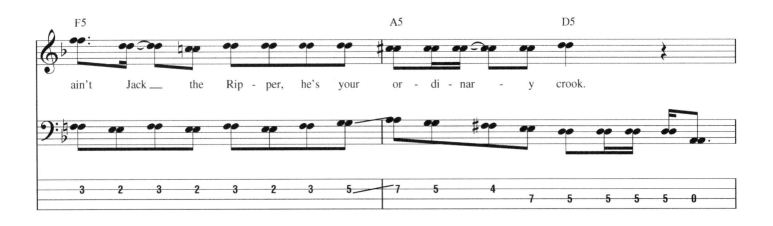

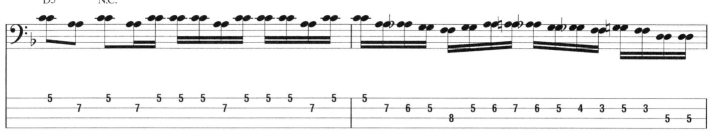

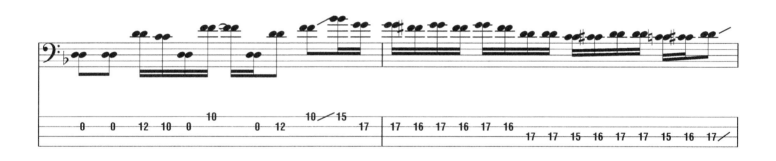
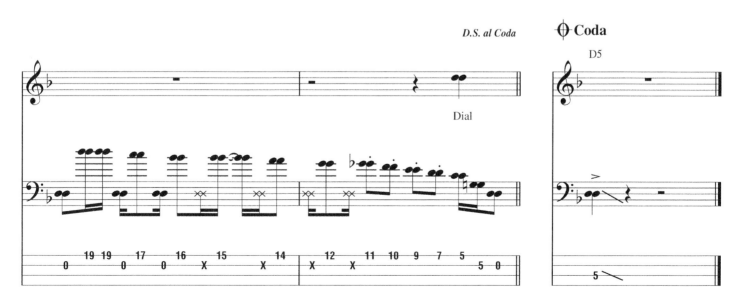

OLD FRIEND

Words and Music by Tim Armstrong,
Matt Freeman and Lars Frederiksen

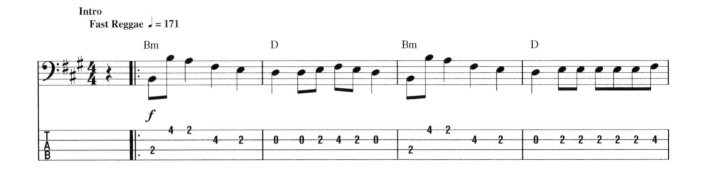
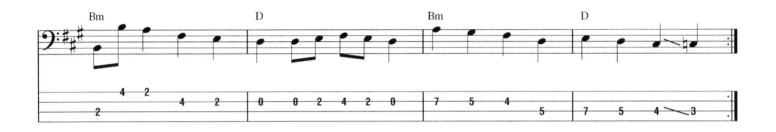

Copyright © 1995 I Want To Go Where The Action Is Music (BMI)
All Rights Administered by Wixen Music Publishing, Inc.
International Copyright Secured   All Rights Reserved

RADIO HAVANA

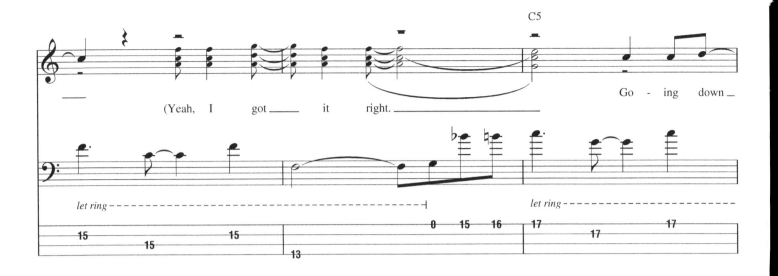
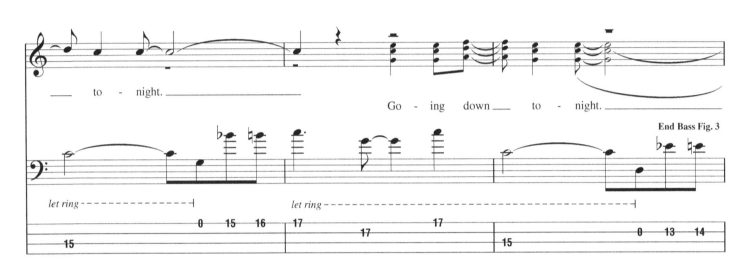

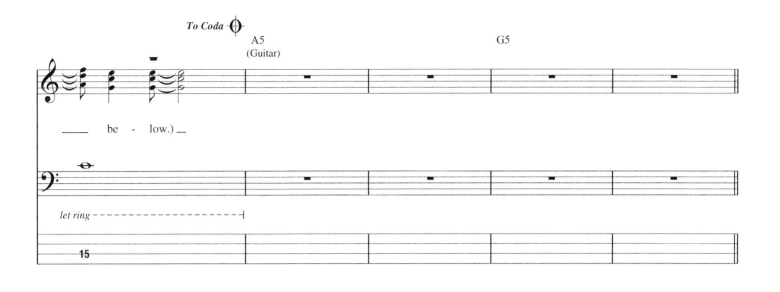
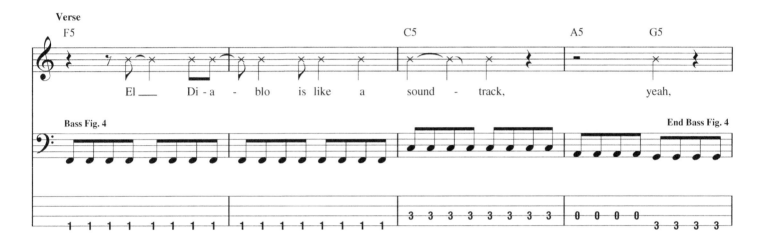
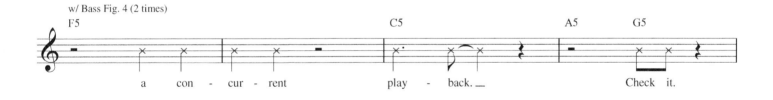
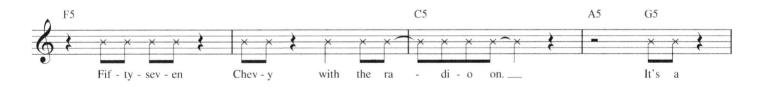
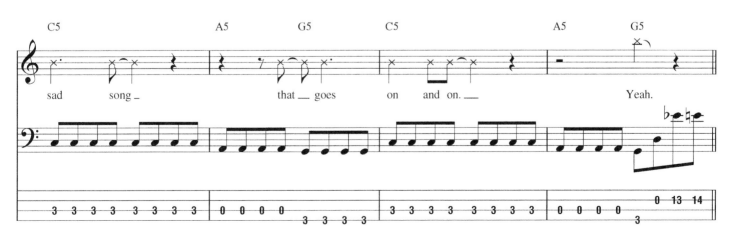

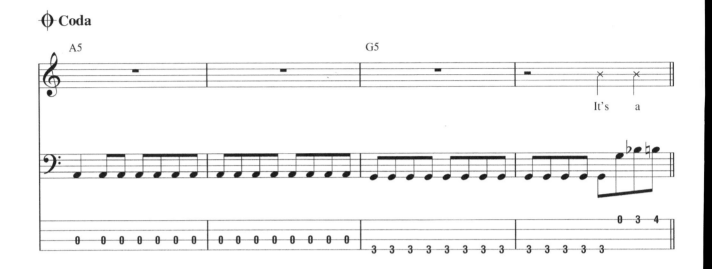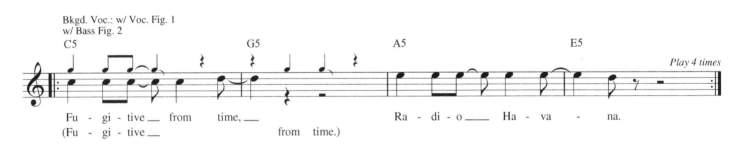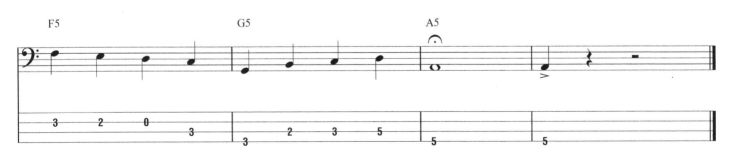

RED HOT MOON

Words and Music by
Tim Armstrong, Lars Frederiksen,
Brett Reed and Rob Aston

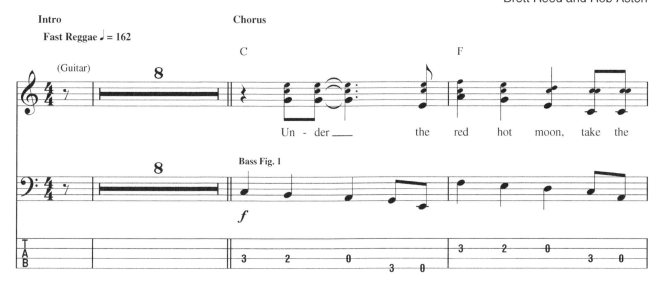

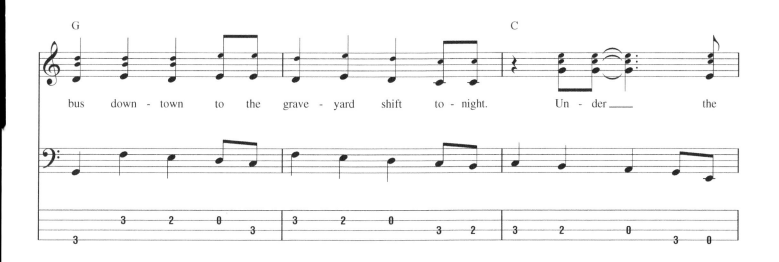

Copyright © 2003 You're A Rattlesnake (ASCAP) and Skinhead Rob Publishing (ASCAP)
All Rights Administered by Wixen Music Publishing, Inc.
International Copyright Secured   All Rights Reserved

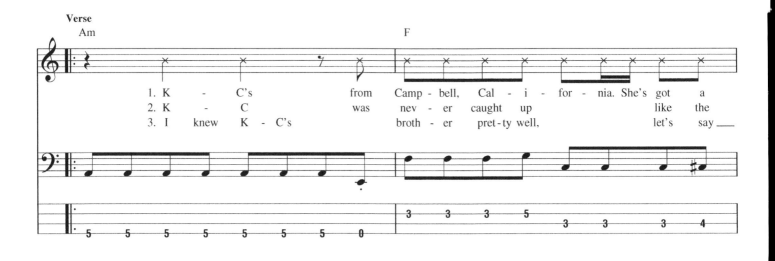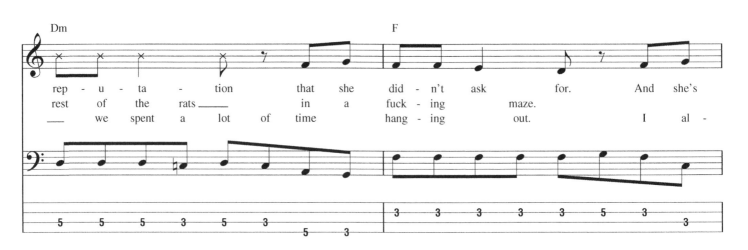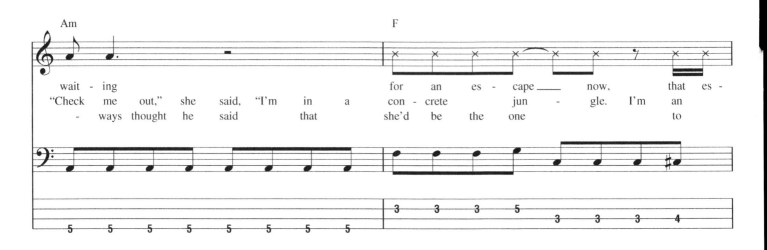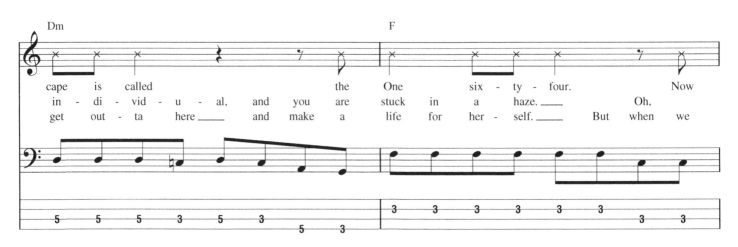

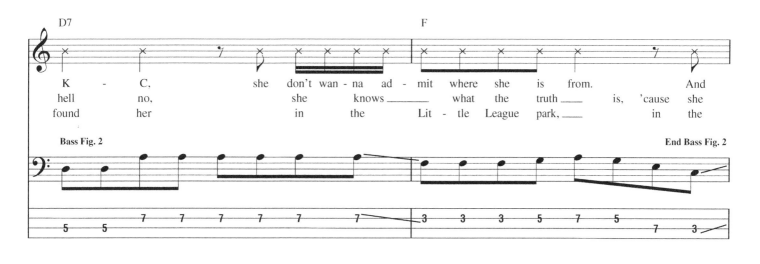
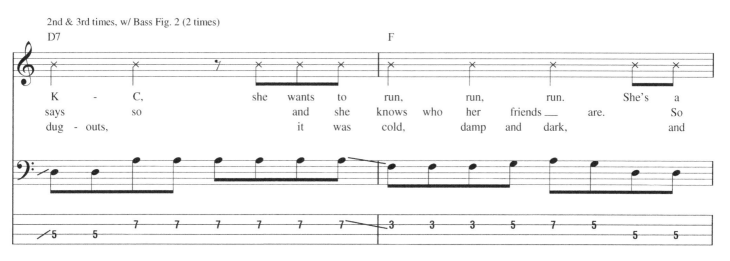

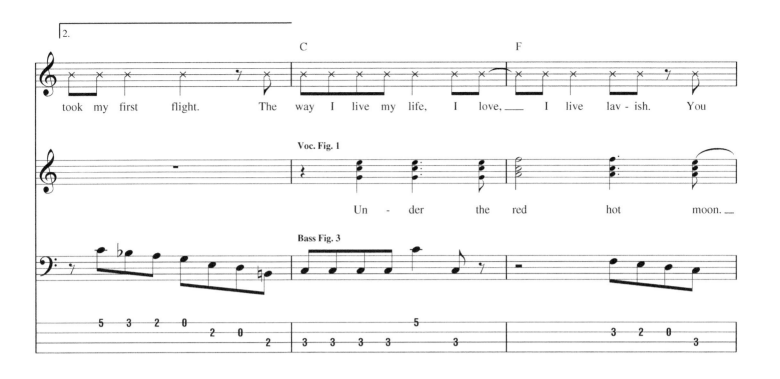
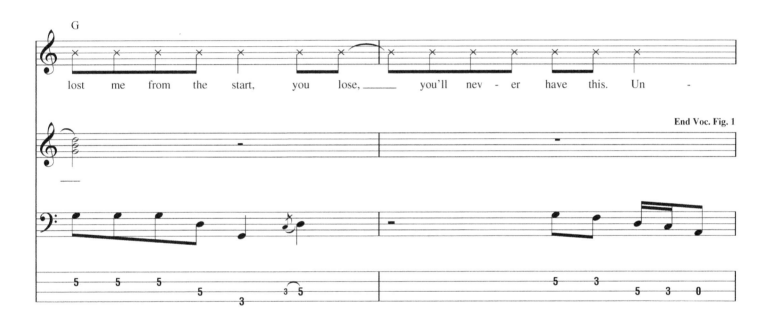
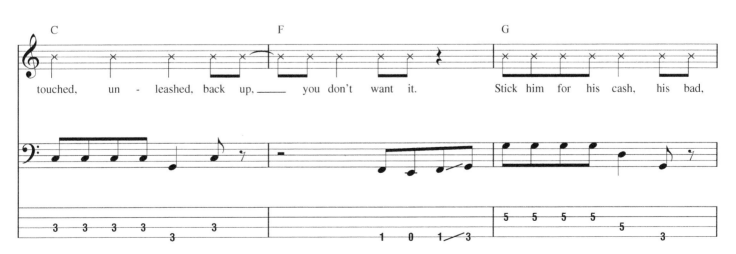

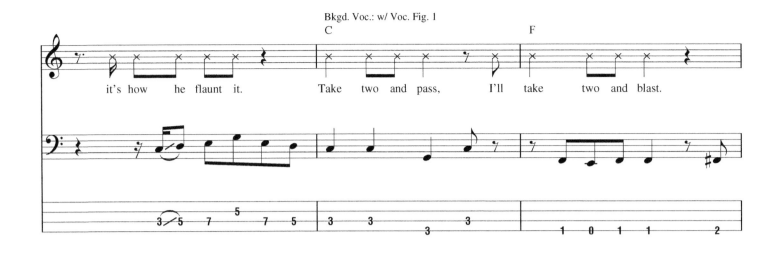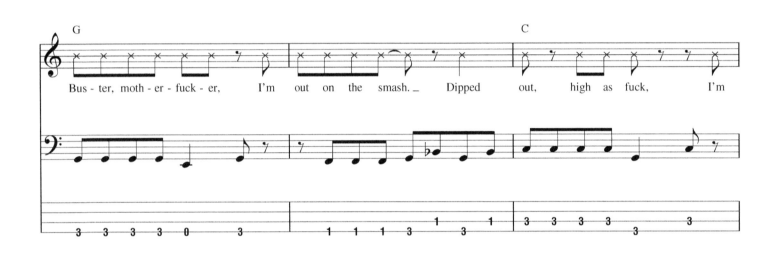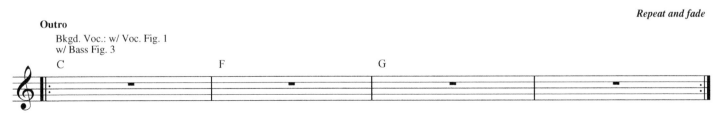

SIDE KICK

Words and Music by
Tim Armstrong and Matt Freeman

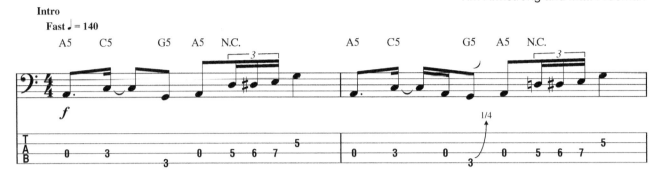
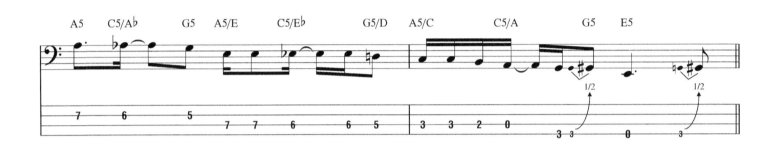
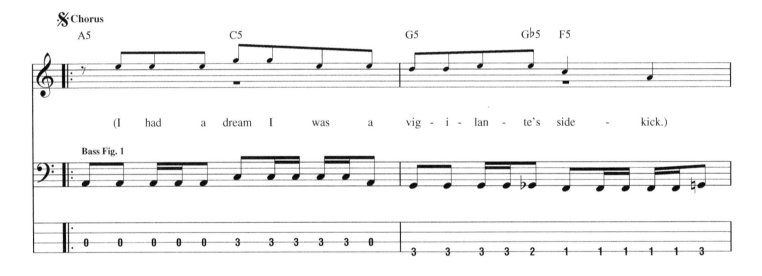

Copyright © 1994 Rancid Music (ASCAP)
All Rights Administered by Wixen Music Publishing, Inc.
International Copyright Secured   All Rights Reserved

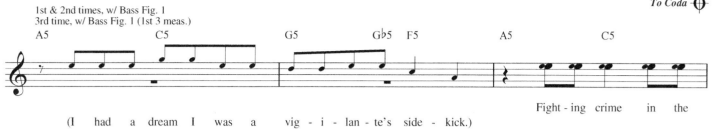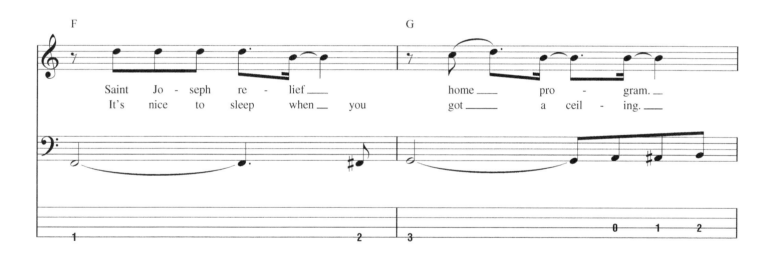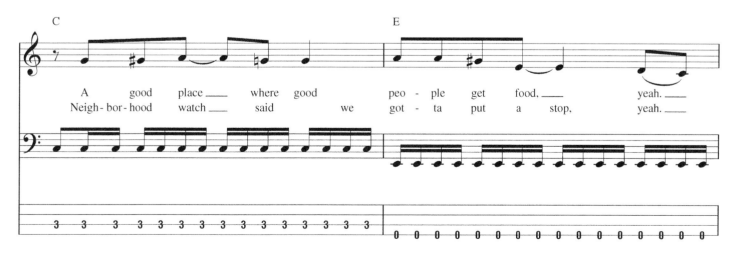

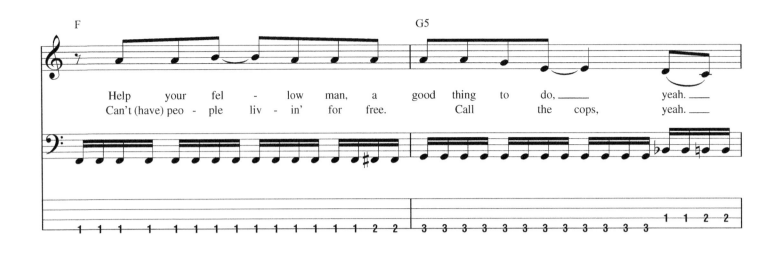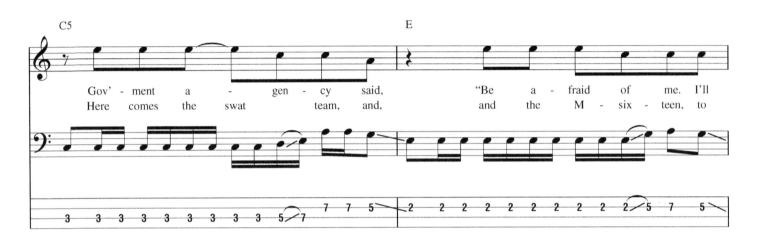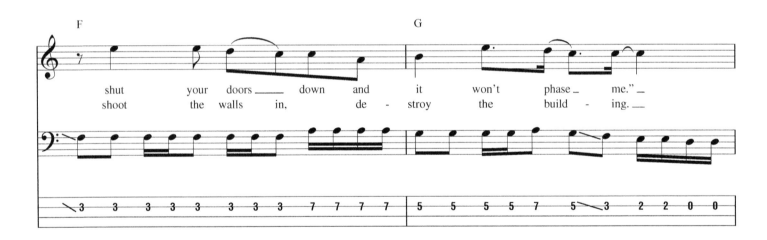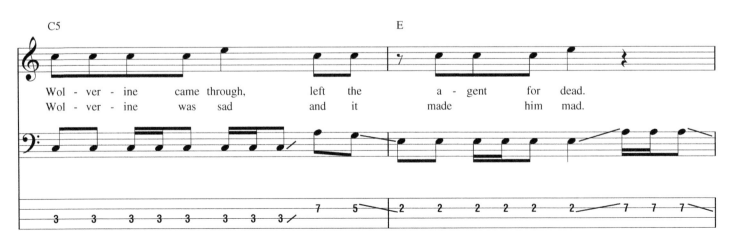

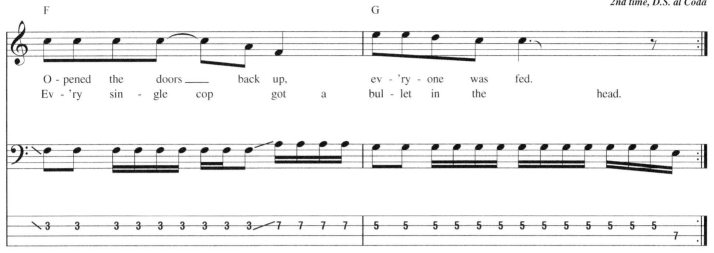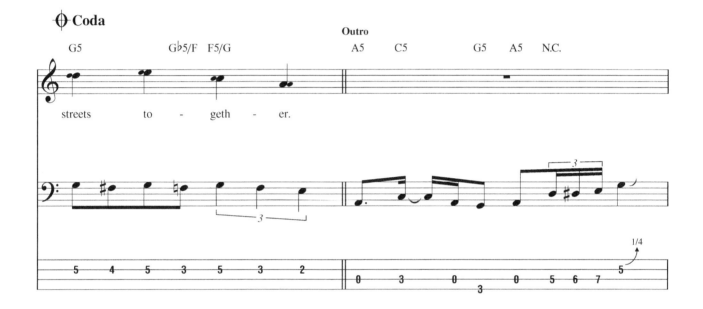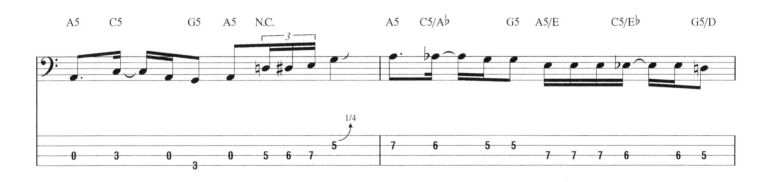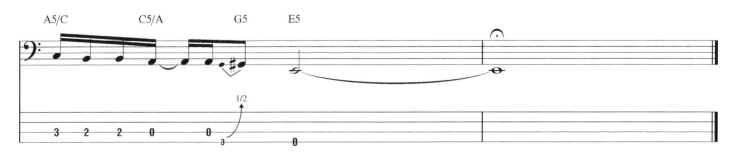

TIME BOMB

Words and Music by Tim Armstrong, Matt Freeman and Lars Frederiksen

Copyright © 1995 I Want To Go Where The Action Is Music (BMI)
All Rights Administered by Wixen Music Publishing, Inc.
International Copyright Secured All Rights Reserved

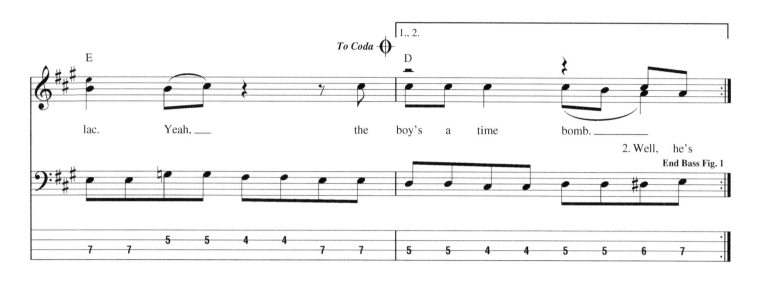
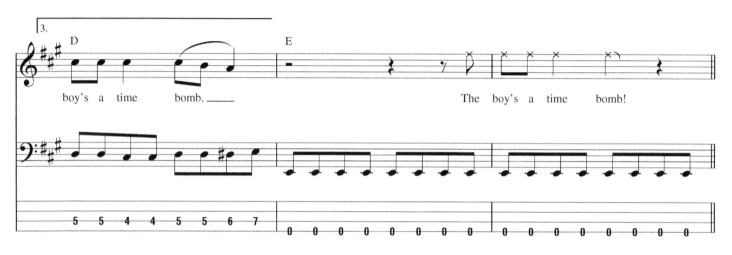

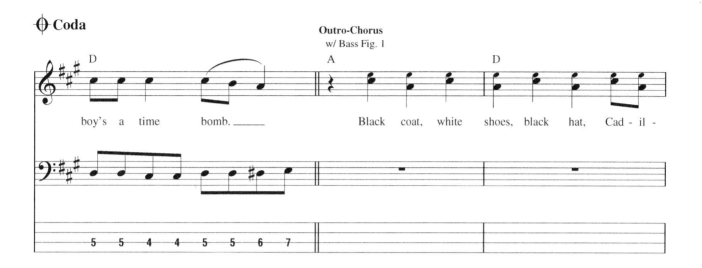

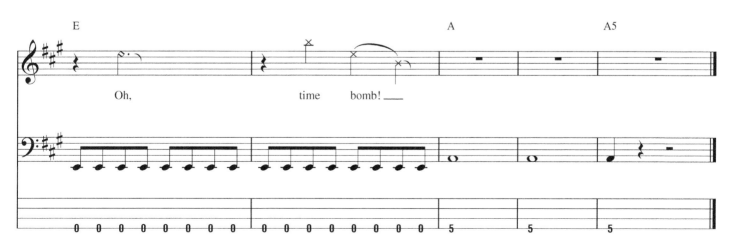

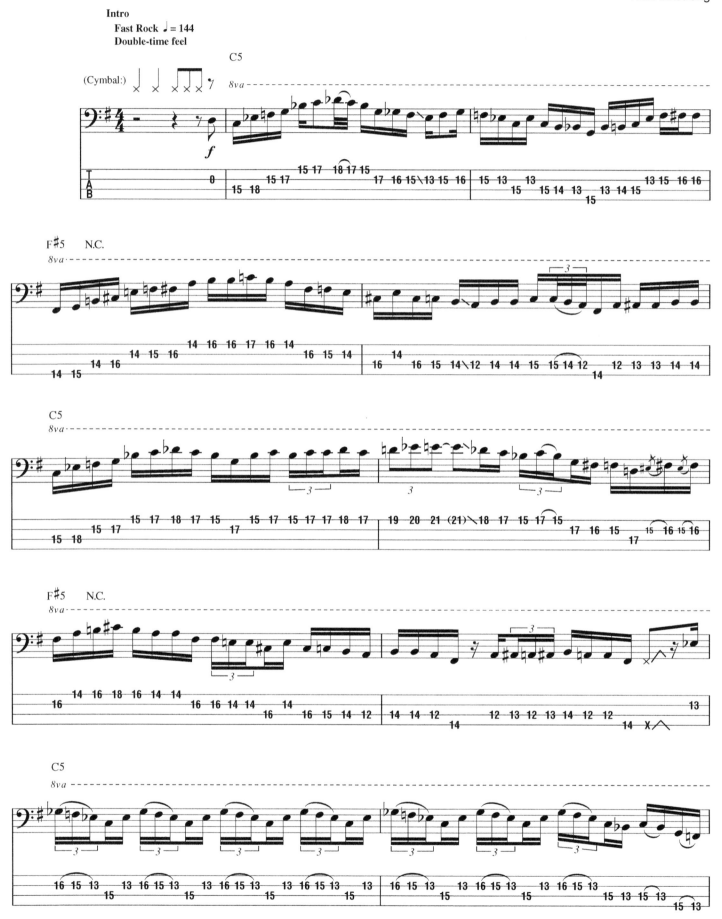

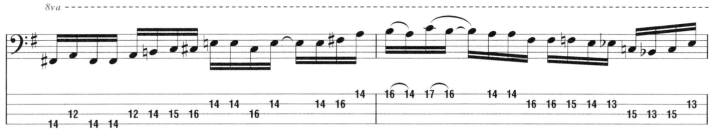
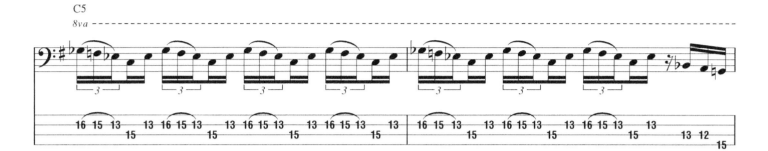
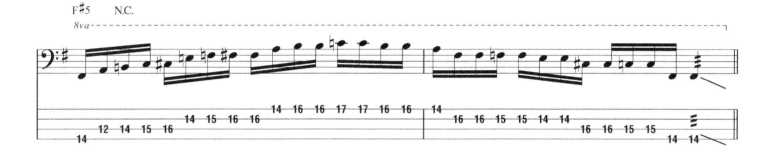
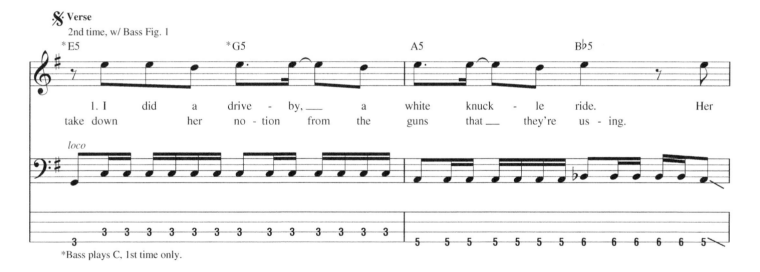
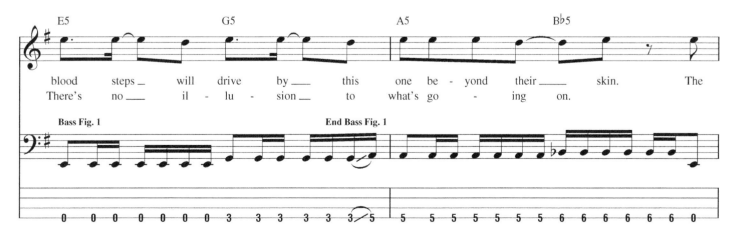

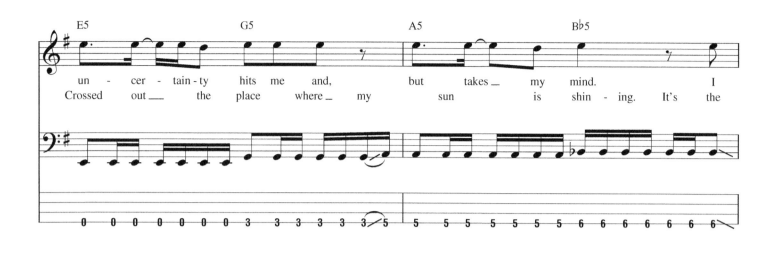
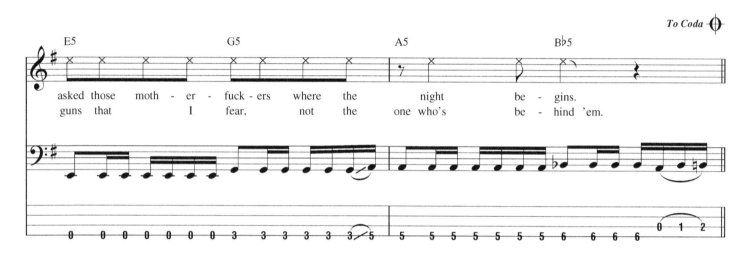
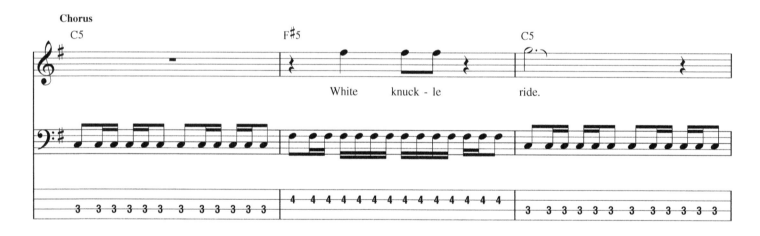
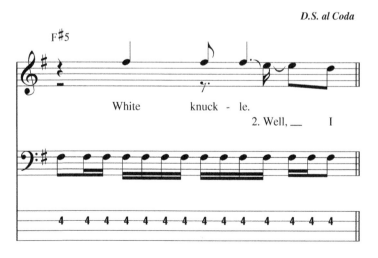
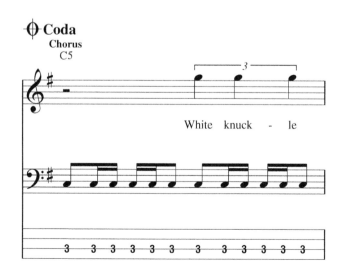

Bass Notation Legend

Bass music can be notated two different ways: on a *musical staff*, and in *tablature*.

THE MUSICAL STAFF shows pitches and rhythms and is divided by bar lines into measures. Pitches are named after the first seven letters of the alphabet.

TABLATURE graphically represents the bass fingerboard. Each horizontal line represents a string, and each number represents a fret.

3rd string, open   2nd string, 2nd fret   1st & 2nd strings open, played together

HAMMER-ON: Strike the first (lower) note with one finger, then sound the higher note (on the same string) with another finger by fretting it without picking.

PULL-OFF: Place both fingers on the notes to be sounded. Strike the first note and without picking, pull the finger off to sound the second (lower) note.

LEGATO SLIDE: Strike the first note and then slide the same fret-hand finger up or down to the second note. The second note is not struck.

SHIFT SLIDE: Same as legato slide, except the second note is struck.

TRILL: Very rapidly alternate between the notes indicated by continuously hammering on and pulling off.

TREMOLO PICKING: The note is picked as rapidly and continuously as possible.

VIBRATO: The string is vibrated by rapidly bending and releasing the note with the fretting hand.

SHAKE: Using one finger, rapidly alternate between two notes on one string by sliding either a half-step above or below.

NATURAL HARMONIC: Strike the note while the fret hand lightly touches the string directly over the fret indicated.

MUFFLED STRINGS: A percussive sound is produced by laying the fret hand across the string(s) without depressing them and striking them with the pick hand.

BEND: Strike the note and bend up the interval shown.

BEND AND RELEASE: Strike the note and bend up as indicated, then release back to the original note. Only the first note is struck.

RIGHT-HAND TAP: Hammer ("tap") the fret indicated with the "pick-hand" index or middle finger and pull off to the note fretted by the fret hand.

LEFT-HAND TAP: Hammer ("tap") the fret indicated with the "fret-hand" index or middle finger.

SLAP: Strike ("slap") string with right-hand thumb.

POP: Snap ("pop") string with right-hand index or middle finger.

Additional Musical Definitions

> (accent)	• Accentuate note (play it louder)		***D.C. al Fine***	• Go back to the beginning of the song and play until the measure marked "***Fine***" (end).
^ (accent)	• Accentuate note with great intensity		**Bass Fig.**	• Label used to recall a recurring pattern.
. (staccato)	• Play the note short		**Fill**	• Label used to identify a brief pattern which is to be inserted into the arrangement.
⊓	• Downstroke		*tacet*	• Instrument is silent (drops out).
V	• Upstroke		‖: :‖	• Repeat measures between signs.
D.S. al Coda	• Go back to the sign (𝄋), then play until the measure marked "***To Coda***," then skip to the section labelled "***Coda***."		1. ‖ 2.	• When a repeated section has different endings, play the first ending only the first time and the second ending only the second time.

NOTE: Tablature numbers in parentheses mean:
1. The note is being sustained over a system (note in standard notation is tied), or
2. The note is sustained, but a new articulation (such as a hammer-on, pull-off, slide or vibrato begins), or
3. The note is a barely audible "ghost" note (note in standard notation is also in parentheses).

80